D0015938

mom's

BOOK OF ANSWERS®

Antoniuk

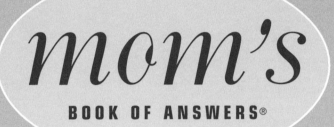

mom's
BOOK OF ANSWERS®

carol bolt

stewart, tabori & chang

new york

Published in 2004 by
Stewart, Tabori & Chang
115 West 18th Street
New York, NY 10011
www.abramsbooks.com

Canadian Distribution:
Canadian Manda Group
One Atlantic Avenue, Suite 105
Toronto, Ontario M6K 3E7
Canada

Library of Congress Cataloging-in-Publication Data

Bolt, Carol, 1963-
          Mom's book of answers / Carol Bolt.
                    p. cm.
               ISBN 1-58479-326-0
1. Fortune-telling by books. 2. Quotations, English-Miscellanea. I. Title

BF1891.B66B649 2004
133.3-dc22

Graphic production by Kim Tyner
Cover and book design by Alexandra Maldonado

Printed and bound in Singapore

10 9 8 7 6 5 4

Stewart, Tabori & Chang is a subsidiary of

LA MARTINIÈRE
GROUPE

What would Mom say?

The Book of Answers® series follows the practice of bibliomancy, or foretelling the future with books. *Mom's Book of Answers* draws advice from that ancient wellspring of hard-won wisdom—other moms. Whether you're seeking guidance about a specific parenting problem, or you just need that maternal point of view for yourself, the solution—from moms through the ages—is channeled through this prophetic guide.

- Hold the book closed and meditate on your query or dilemma. Your question can be as long or as short as you like.

- As you riffle the pages from back to front with your thumb, ask yourself, "What would Mom say?" When you feel the time is right, stop, and open the book to the page where your thumb came to rest: There is your answer.

wait until your father gets home

don't talk with your mouth full

wash your hands first

don't push

excuse yourself from the room

give it a rest

finish what's on your plate

Yes, of course,
after you've finished all
your chores

visit your mother once in a while

is there anything you've forgotten?

you can only control your
own actions

give it some time

cover your mouth

not in your good clothes

there's nothing more to say about it

you get what you ask for

do as I say, not as I do

don't start something you can't finish

don't dwell on what you can't have

finish what is right in front
of you first

try it, you'll like it

you can do anything you set
your mind to

nothing lasts forever

let someone know
that you got there safely

what would Grandma say about that?

if you do it the way you've always done it,
you'll get what you've always gotten

make a good impression

slow down

hurry up

that's nice, dear

nothing's perfect

don't fuss about it

you'll get what's coming to you

you'll catch more flies with honey than vinegar

use your common sense

don't cry over spilled milk

there's a helping hand at the
end of your arm

**you must have something better
to do than that**

don't let your alligator mouth get you in trouble

don't waste your time wondering,
get busy and do it

sit there until you are calm about it

if all your friends jumped off a bridge
would you do that too?

yes, dear

**if that's what you think,
you've got another think coming**

you can have dessert after you eat
all of your vegetables

you've been told a million times,
don't exaggerate

be careful,
you don't know where it's been

don't put it in your mouth

look but don't touch

listen: Mother knows best

things are never as bad as they seem

what you need is a home-cooked meal

don't make up stories

better to be seen and not heard

you need a nap

tell someone all about it

save it for a rainy day

spend your money on something that will last

this, too, shall pass

what's the big hurry?

nobody said it was going to be easy

you can't undo what's been done

be careful what you ask for,
you just might get it

if you're in doubt about what to do,
go clean something

may you have children just like you

be your own best friend

if you don't decide,
it'll get decided for you

use your words

everything's going to be all right

be careful

go ask your father

wait until you're married

share with others

go to your room

say thank you

say please

if you don't have anything nice to say,
don't say anything at all

get a good night's sleep

if you're not careful you could
get stuck that way

go outside and play

no . . .
because I said so

you need a hug

if it doesn't work out,
you can always come home

mind your own business

there's always enough time to do the right thing

use moderation

be home by ten o'clock sharp

keep your hair out of your face;
you have such a lovely face,
let it be seen . . . .

sorry, we weren't paying attention;
would you say that again?

you'll understand better when you
have children of your own

you can be your own worst enemy

don't be too hard on yourself

when you're grown up you can do
whatever you want

there are always two sides to a story

no . . . and that's final

take a bath

bake cookies for someone

never test the water with both feet

you can't be listening
if your mouth is moving

stand up straight

when faced with
choices A and B,
choose C

what goes around comes around

be thankful for what you have

don't worry about things that haven't happened yet

you're responsible for
your own happiness

it may come back to haunt you

wear a hat,
a scarf,
gloves,
extra socks,
and boots . . .

do what you want to be seen doing on the front page of tomorrow's paper

clean up after yourself

your actions will speak louder
than your words

just relax, be yourself

what do you think you're doing?

**remember,
no matter what you decide,
your mom always loves you**

**the privileges that you've earned
can be taken away**

everything has a price

don't make excuses

don't make me come over there

you're grounded

don't complain; in the old days,
we walked five miles in the snow
just to get the mail,
and that was before breakfast . . .

there are more important things
to worry about

not everything is about you

take a little time out

do you have on clean underwear?

everything you need will be right here

be what you want to be

have enough sense to come in out of the rain

cross that bridge when you come to it

you sure do ask a lot of questions

you're going to need your strength

not at someone else's expense

some things will be better left unsaid

make your mom proud

turn "shoulds" into "coulds"

**please ask again,
using your indoor voice**

don't rush into anything

it'll all come out in the wash

play nicely

there's no reason to get upset

wait your turn

read a book, it'll make you a more interesting person

don't worry about what others think

nobody ever said life would be fair, easy, or fun

wait until your father gets home

don't talk with your mouth full

wash your hands first

don't push

excuse yourself from the room

give it a rest

finish what's on your plate

Yes, of course,
after you've finished all
your chores

visit your mother once in a while

is there anything you've forgotten?

you can only control your
own actions

give it some time

cover your mouth

not in your good clothes

there's nothing more to say about it

you get what you ask for

do as I say, not as I do

don't start something you can't finish

don't dwell on what you can't have

finish what is right in front
of you first

try it, you'll like it

you can do anything you set
your mind to

nothing lasts forever

**let someone know
that you got there safely**

what would Grandma say about that?

if you do it the way you've always done it,
you'll get what you've always gotten

make a good impression

slow down

that's nice, dear

nothing's perfect

don't fuss about it

you'll get what's coming to you

you'll catch more flies with honey than vinegar

use your common sense

don't cry over spilled milk

there's a helping hand at the end of your arm

you must have something better
to do than that

don't let your alligator mouth get you in trouble

don't waste your time wondering,
get busy and do it

sit there until you are calm about it

if all your friends jumped off a bridge would you do that too?

yes, dear

if that's what you think,
you've got another think coming

you can have dessert after you eat
all of your vegetables

you've been told a million times,
don't exaggerate

**be careful,
you don't know where it's been**

don't put it in your mouth

look but don't touch

listen: Mother knows best

things are never as bad as they seem

what you need is a home-cooked meal

don't make up stories

better to be seen and not heard

you need a nap

tell someone all about it

save it for a rainy day

spend your money on something
that will last

this, too, shall pass

what's the big hurry?

nobody said it was going to be easy

you can't undo what's been done

be careful what you ask for,
you just might get it

if you're in doubt about what to do,
go clean something

may you have children just like you

be your own best friend

**if you don't decide,
it'll get decided for you**

use your words

everything's going to be all right

be careful

go ask your father

wait until you're married

share with others

go to your room

say thank you

say please

if you don't have anything nice to say,
don't say anything at all

get a good night's sleep

if you're not careful you could get stuck that way

go outside and play

no . . .
because I said so

you need a hug

if it doesn't work out,
you can always come home

mind your own business

there's always enough time to do the right thing

use moderation

be home by ten o'clock sharp

keep your hair out of your face;
you have such a lovely face,
let it be seen . . . .

sorry, we weren't paying attention;
would you say that again?

you'll understand better when you
have children of your own

you can be your own worst enemy

don't be too hard on yourself

when you're grown up you can do whatever you want

there are always two sides to a story

no . . . and that's final

take a bath

bake cookies for someone

never test the water with both feet

you can't be listening
if your mouth is moving

stand up straight

when faced with
choices A and B,
choose C

what goes around comes around

be thankful for what you have

don't worry about things that haven't happened yet

**you're responsible for
your own happiness**

it may come back to haunt you

wear a hat,
a scarf,
gloves,
extra socks,
and boots . . .

do what you want to be seen doing on the front page of tomorrow's paper

clean up after yourself

your actions will speak louder
than your words

just relax, be yourself

what do you think you're doing?

**do the right thing;
not what's the easiest, prettiest,
or most popular**

the privileges that you've earned
can be taken away

everything has a price

don't make excuses

don't make me come over there

you're grounded

don't complain; in the old days,
we walked five miles in the snow
just to get the mail,
and that was before breakfast...

there are more important things
to worry about

not everything is about you

take a little time out

do you have on clean underwear?

everything you need will be right here

be what you want to be

have enough sense to come in out
of the rain

cross that bridge when you come to it

you sure do ask a lot of questions

you're going to need your strength

not at someone else's expense

some things will be better left unsaid

make your mom proud

turn "shoulds" into "coulds"

please ask again,
using your indoor voice

don't rush into anything

it'll all come out in the wash

play nicely

there's no reason to get upset

wait your turn

read a book, it'll make you a more interesting person

don't worry about what others think,
just do your own thing

nobody ever said life would be fair, easy, or fun

everything's going to be all right

Acknowledgments

This book is dedicated to my Mom, Doris Anderson Bolt. I didn't always understand the pearls of wisdom you shared with me when I was a kid, but like so many other adults, I do now! I also know that it was tough, but just between us; of the two boys and one girl you raised, I was the easy one, right? (Just kidding; I know the truth.) Thank you, Mom.

I would also like to thank my birth mother. While I never actually met you, you gave me two of the most special gifts anyone can give: you brought me into this world and then adopted me into a family that was able to give me a life. I know this couldn't have been easy. Thank you.

Thank you to my agents, Victoria Sanders and Chandler Crawford—you both are amazing. You keep finding new doors for me to step through, and I am truly grateful.

Cheers and gratitude to Stewart, Tabori & Chang: publisher Leslie Stoker; editor Anne Kostick; book designers Alexandra Maldonado and Galen Smith; production director Kim Tyner; and publicist Caroline Enright. Thank you for giving me the opportunity to have the job I've always dreamed of—making books.

And of course, mountains of thanks to my friends who emailed, phoned, and laughed while updating me on their latest my-mom-used-to-say remembrances: Basha Brownstein, Kris Caldwell, Aileen Gagney, Bill Grace, and Benee Knauer. Sorry pals, a few of those weren't appropriate for printing, but I sure did enjoy hearing them!